Helen T. Foui

CORSICA TRAVEL GUIDE UNVEILED 2024

The Most Completed Pocket Guide to Discover Corsica Hidden Treasure

Table of Contents

This page was left blank intentionally

Introduction

Welcome to Corsica, the island of contrasts and charm. This hidden jewel in the midst of the Mediterranean is a haven for people looking for a unique blend of history, culture, and natural beauties.

Corsica, also known as the "Island of Beauty," has a diverse scenery that ranges from rough mountains to exquisite beaches. The aroma of the maquis, a fragrant blend of plants and wildflowers, fills the air as you weave your way through the twisting roads, which reveal beautiful vistas at every bend.

As you step onto this sun-kissed land, you'll find yourself immersed in a cultural mosaic shaped by centuries of influence from various civilizations. The history of the island is inscribed in its old citadels, Genoese castles, and picturesque villages, each of which tells a story of resistance and a distinct Corsican character.

Corsica, on the other hand, is a living, breathing painting of the present. The inhabitants, who are known for their friendliness and hospitality, will greet you with open arms. Engaging in a leisurely chat with a café owner while sipping a cup of powerful Corsican coffee can transform you from a visitor to a participant in the island's dynamic everyday life.

Corsica is a playground of outdoor activities for the brave. Hike the renowned GR20 trail, a difficult but rewarding hike across rugged peaks and lush forests. If the sea calls, enjoy the underwater delights of the Mediterranean by exploring secluded coves and crystal-clear waters.

Of course, no trip to Corsica is complete without sampling the island's delectable cuisine. The tables of local restaurants are adorned with savory charcuterie, artisanal cheeses, and fine seafood, encouraging you to experience the authentic flavors of the island.

So, whether you're interested in history, nature, or new culinary experiences, Corsica welcomes you with open arms. Prepare for an out-of-the-ordinary experience, where every moment is a brushstroke on the canvas of your extraordinary voyage. Enjoy your stay in this captivating blend of tradition and modernity, where Corsica's essence awaits discovery.

History and Culture

Let's go back in time to ancient times. Corsica's history reads like an epic novel. It was inhabited by a variety of peoples, including Etruscans and Greeks, who left their imprint on the island. In 238 BC, the Romans assumed power, always looking for strategic positions. After then, there were the Vandals, the Byzantines, and even a brief period of Moorish dominance.

Things start to get fascinating in the Middle Ages. Corsica becomes a point of dispute between the Republics of Genoa and Pisa. These Italian city-states competed with one another for the coolest piece of real estate. Genoa gained the prize after a tug of battle, and Corsica became a Genoese territory in the 15th century.

Corsicans, being the proud people that they are, were dissatisfied with Genoese authority. The island had multiple revolts and wars, with Pasquale Paoli being one of the most noteworthy personalities. This man was a Corsican hero who ruled the Corsican Republic in the 18th century. But, hey, nothing lasts forever, and Corsica became a part of France in 1769.

Return to the twentieth century. Corsica experienced ups and downs throughout WWII, and there was a resurgence of Corsican nationalism following the war. The yearning for independence and the preservation of Corsican culture became prominent.

Let's now shift our focus to the cultural realm. Corsican culture is a web of influences. Corsu is a romance language with a distinct taste. Music is important, and Corsican tunes cannot be discussed without including polyphonic singing. It's like shiver-inducing vocal acrobatics.

Corsicans take their festivities quite seriously. In Bonifacio, the Festival of Saint John is a spectacle, with inhabitants lighting bonfires and diving into the sea to purify themselves. If you like horseback riding, the Cargese festival includes the "Maiu," a great equestrian event.

Let us not forget about food. Corsican cuisine is a delicious feast for the senses. They know how to satisfy the palate with everything from wild boar specialties to delectable cheeses. Let's not even get started on the Corsican wines. Sip a glass with a view of the Calanques and you'll understand what I mean.

Corsica is a mix of ancient history, hardy people, breathtaking landscapes, and a culture that is as diverse as it is compelling. It's a Mediterranean treasure that has endured through the years. So, if you ever find yourself on this island of opposites, prepare to be charmed by a voyage through time and culture.

What Sets Corsica Apart as a Unique Travel Destination

A Tapestry of History:

Corsica's history is a mosaic of influences. Each culture, from the ancient Greeks to the Romans, the Pisans to the Genoese, has weaved its threads into the fabric of Corsican identity. Battles and alliances have occurred on the island, leaving behind a magnificent tapestry of fortifications, citadels, and lovely villages that say volumes about its stubborn past.

Corsican Food:

Prepare your taste senses for a culinary symphony. Corsican cuisine combines French and Italian influences with a splash of local flavor. Don't pass up the brocciu, a unique Corsican cheese that can be found in both savory and sweet recipes. Of course, a taste of local wine is a salute to the island's sun-kissed vineyards.

Scenic Diversity:

Corsica is a natural wonder. The island's varied landscape runs from the steep peaks of the interior—home to Corsica's highest peak, Monte Cinto—to the lovely beaches that line the coast. Corsica's landscapes offer a spectacular spectacle for hikers, beachgoers, and nature lovers alike.

A Language of Its Own:

Corsican, a Romance language with Italian roots, exemplifies the island's cultural independence. While French is frequently spoken, hearing Corsican in the marketplaces and tiny streets adds a real element to the experience, making you feel as if you've entered a world where time moves at a different pace.

Festivals and Traditions:

Corsican festivals celebrate life and heritage. The Festival of Saint Erasmus, with its colorful processions and marine traditions, symbolizes Corsica's close relationship with the sea. Immerse yourself in music festivals where polyphonic singing takes center stage and resonates through historic alleyways.

The Corsican Way of Life:

Corsicans take pride in their relaxed way of life. Time appears to slow down, beckoning you to cherish each moment. Corsica invites you to adopt a more tranquil pace, leaving the rush and bustle behind, whether it's sitting over a lunch with locals or discovering secret coves.

Corsica is more than just a place to visit; it's an experience that goes beyond the standard travel tale. Its history, cuisine, landscapes, language, festivals, and way of life all come together to create a destination that should be lived rather than just visited. It's a location where every day is a page in a novel that you become a part of—an island that not only captures your senses but also inscribes itself on your spirit.

Geography and Climate

Corsica is a rough and diversified treasure in the center of the Mediterranean. Its scenery is a work of art, with towering mountains, lush woods, and exquisite beaches. The towering grandeur of the Corsican Alps dominates the island, with Monte Cinto proudly standing as the tallest summit, reaching over 8,800 feet. The rugged topography gives way to deep gorges, making it a hiking and wildlife enthusiast's paradise.

As you travel throughout the island, you'll come across charming communities clinging to mountain peaks and surrounded by vineyards and olive trees. The coastal areas, with their beautiful cliffs and secluded bays, offer a striking contrast to the inland environment.

Corsica is endowed with immense natural beauty that showcases the island's distinct blend of French and Italian influences. Corsicans have retained their heritage and traditions, giving cultural richness to the already stunning landscape.

Corsica's climate is a harmonious harmony that entices tourists all year. Summers are hot and dry, luring beachgoers to the pristine beaches. Consider yourself lazing in the Mediterranean sun, the azure seas gently lapping at your feet.

Spring and autumn present a welcome shift, with cooler temperatures that make trekking and exploring the hilly landscapes ideal. Corsica's different microclimates provide an element of surprise, making each visit a one-of-a-kind experience.

Corsica's winters, however mild in comparison to Europe as a whole add to the island's tranquillity. Snow-capped peaks provide a stunning backdrop, and the snug mountain settlements emanate a warmth that contrasts with the chilly air.

Corsica's climate caters to a wide range of preferences, whether you prefer the sun or the snow. Because of the island's geographical diversity, each region has its own individual weather patterns, allowing visitors to choose their ideal environment and experience Corsica in a way that is meaningful to them.

Corsica's geography and climate, in essence, weave a dynamic tapestry that unfolds as you explore this Mediterranean jewel. Corsica offers a story of nature's grandeur and human perseverance from the summits of its mountains to the shores of its beaches, making it a must-visit destination for travelers seeking a mix of adventure, peacefulness, and cultural richness.

Cultural Etiquette: Tips for Respectful Travel

Corsica is proud of its rich cultural legacy, which is strongly steeped in traditions. Respect for local customs is welcomed while interacting with them. Corsicans value close-knit communities, and visitors who embrace local norms often discover friendliness. In the afternoon and evening, it is usual to greet with a friendly "Bun di" (Good day) and "Sera" (Evening).

Corsica's calendar is filled with vivid festivals that represent the island's dynamic culture. The well-known Carnival of Corsica, which takes place in February, is a dazzling exhibition of colorful parades, traditional costumes, and vibrant music. These events provide insight into the island's history, mythology, and people's spirit.

The family is the foundation of Corsican society. Locals frequently congregate for extended family gatherings, showing their hospitality through a variety of wonderful delicacies. Respect for family relationships is essential, and tourists who embrace this familial attitude frequently discover a welcome atmosphere.

"paghjella," or Corsican polyphonic singing, is a UNESCO-listed intangible cultural property. This intriguing musical heritage embodies the history and soul of the island. Visitors can immerse themselves in the musical appeal of Corsican music by enjoying impromptu street performances or attending local concerts.

While French is commonly spoken, Corsican (Corsu) is the native language and has cultural significance. Visitors who make an effort to acquire a few basic Corsican words are appreciated by the locals. Simple greetings and expressions can help develop friendships and demonstrate a genuine interest in the local culture.

Corsicans take pride in their appearance, and informal yet well-dressed attire is often preferred. As a symbol of respect, slightly more formal clothes is recommended when attending religious or cultural activities.

While Corsica is a photographer's dream, it's crucial to respect the privacy of the residents. Always obtain permission before photographing someone, especially in rural towns and villages where privacy is greatly prized.

It is usual to bring a small gift as a gesture of thanks when invited to a Corsican home. Take your time at meals and consume the local delicacies. Engage in conversation, and don't be shocked if a lunch lasts many hours; it's a testament to the island's laid-back lifestyle.

Travelers can form genuine friendships and truly experience the essence of Corsican life by embracing these cultural subtleties.

Visa And Travel Requirement

Before the flight, each passenger must ensure that they have valid travel documents that meet with the provisions of Immigration Services, and the authorities of the destination countries.

We recommend that you contact the appropriate embassies or consulates to check the entry and travel requirements for your destination country/countries. All travelers, including babies and minors, must travel with appropriate travel documentation.

A valid National Identity Card issued by an EU government or a Schengen Agreement signatory. Germany, Austria, Belgium, Bulgaria, Cyprus, Denmark, Spain, Estonia, Finland, France, Greece, Hungary, Ireland, Iceland, Italy, Latvia, Liechtenstein, Lithuania, Luxembourg, Malta, Norway, The Netherlands, Poland, Portugal, United Kingdom, Czech Republic, Slovak Republic, Romania, Slovenia, Sweden, and Switzerland are among the countries mentioned.

A driving license, but only for flights within France's urban area.

All travel beyond the European Economic Area (EEA) necessitates the use of a passport that is valid for the period of the intended stay.

If necessary, a visa. It is the responsibility of each passenger to check the validity date of their travel documents and, if required, renew them (please keep in mind that this may take some time).

Temporary documents issued for the purpose of obtaining a National Identity Card or Passport are not permitted. This is due to the absence of a photograph in these documents.

The French National Identity Card is now valid for 15 years, rather than 10 years, as of January 2014. Cards issued prior to this date have a 5-year extension after their initial validity period. Nonetheless, some countries (like Belgium) reject the new clause. We also strongly advise you to travel with a valid passport in order to meet the entry and stay criteria of your destination country.

Some countries demand a passport that is valid for at least six months after the date of return. In addition, a ticket for the return voyage or onward travel may be necessary.

Please keep in mind that some nations mandate airlines to give part or all of the information they have about their passengers. The relevant information appears in the encoded areas of the passport.

20 THINGS TO KNOW ABOUT CORSICA

If you are considering Corsica for your next walking vacation, you should learn more about this lovely and fascinating island.

1. After Cyprus, Sardinia, and Sicily, Corsica is the fourth largest island in the Mediterranean Sea.
2. Despite its location between Italy's west coast and the north coast of Sardinia (an Italian island), the island is French.
3. In 1768, Corsica was ceded to France, which sits to the island's north-west.
4. Napoleon Bonaparte was born a year later in Ajaccio (Ajax), one of Corsica's largest towns, in 1769. He was born into an affluent family and was sent to military school near Troyes in northern France at the age of nine.
5. Corsica is commonly referred to be one of France's 26 regions, but in law it is a territorial collectivity, which means it has significantly greater power than other French regions.

6. The other three important settlements on the island are Corte, Bastia and Sartene.

7. The island is divided into two departments: Corse-du-Sud and Haute-Corse.

8. The main towns of Corsica include Ajaccio, which is also known by its Latin name of Ajax.

9. Although French is the official language of Corsica, Corsican (Corsu) is also spoken and taught in schools.

10. 10. Corsica boasts 1,000 kilometers of coastline, with beaches accounting for one-third of it.

11. There are over 200 beaches on the island, with Calvi Beach in the north-west being one of the nicest.

12. The island is also quite mountainous, with the highest peak of Monte Cinto standing at 2,706 meters, about double the height of Ben Nevis in the United Kingdom. There are another 20 2,000-meter peaks.

13. The Parc Naturel Regional de Corse, established in 1972 on the island, protects thousands of rare animal and plant species.

14. Calanches de Piana is a UNESCO World Heritage Site that is part of the regional park.

15. Lariccio pine trees, sometimes known as Corsican pines, are indigenous to the island. Some trees have been found to be 500 years old.

16. Corsica's numerous Genoese bridges are a major tourist attraction. They are made of stone and have a humped arc with a narrow highway.

17. The climate is Mediterranean, with hot, dry summers and warm, rainy winters. There are, however, parts of the island that have varied "microclimates" depending on altitude.

18. The climate is typically Mediterranean, with hot dry summers and mild yet rainy winters. There are, however, parts of the island that have varied "microclimates" depending on altitude.

19. Corsica's climate is perfect for making wine yet few people from outside the island will get their hands on a bottle. This is because the majority of the wine, which is usually red and made from the niellucciu and sciaccarellu grapes, is consumed by the island's population.

20. Brocciu (cheese), Figatellu (pork), Fiaddone (cheese cake), and Miel (honey) are traditional Corsican foods.

Transportation

1. Renting a Car:

Corsica is best explored at your own time, and renting a car allows you to explore the island's twisting roads and hidden treasures. Driving allows you to see rural villages and gorgeous coastal routes, thanks to well-maintained roadways and scenic coastal routes. Prepare for tight mountain roads; a smaller vehicle may be more practicable.

2. Public Transportation:

The island's public transportation infrastructure, mainly buses and railroads, is dependable, connecting major villages and cities. Buses are a low-cost choice, but schedules might change, so it's best to prepare beforehand. Trains provide a magnificent tour across the interior of the island, exhibiting its natural splendor.

3. Taxis and Ride-Sharing:

Taxis are frequently available in cities and near important tourist attractions. Ride-sharing services may be limited, so check local rules first. Taxis are a good option for short journeys or when you don't want to drive.

5. Air Travel:

Consider domestic flights if you're pressed for time. Corsica has many airports, the most important of which are in Ajaccio, Bastia, and Calvi. Flights from mainland France are regular, making it a quick and easy method to get to the island.

6. Walking and Cycling:

Exploring on foot or by bicycle in towns and cities is a delightful way to absorb the local atmosphere. Many areas are walkable, and riding allows you to explore picturesque alleys and hidden courtyards.

Tips for Renting a car in Corsica

1. Make a Reservation in Advance:

It's best to reserve your rental car ahead of time, especially during peak tourist seasons. This not only assures that you get the vehicle of your choosing, but it also generally results in lower rates.

2. Choose the Right Size:

Corsica's roads can be winding and narrow, particularly in mountainous regions. Choose a smaller vehicle that can easily negotiate these roads. Furthermore, smaller cars are easier to park in congested city centers.

3. Check Rental Policies:

Read the rental policies carefully before finalizing your reservation. Take note of any fuel rules, mileage limits, and additional expenses. This prevents surprises when returning the vehicle.

4. International Driving Permit:

While not necessarily required, obtaining an International Driving Permit can be beneficial, especially if you intend to go to remote places. Check with your rental agent for precise regulations.

5. Be familiar with Corsican roads:

Corsican roads can be difficult to navigate, with steep inclines and hairpin curves. Drive with caution, especially in mountainous areas. Take your time admiring the scenery and be cautious of local traffic laws.

6. Fill Up in Bigger Cities:

In some rural locations, gas stations can be scarce. To avoid running out of petrol in more isolated regions, it's a good idea to top up your tank in larger towns.

7. GPS and Maps

While GPS is useful, having a printed map can be invaluable, especially if you are in an area with poor satellite reception. Before you leave, familiarize yourself with your route.

8. Respect Parking Rules:

Parking laws in Corsica's cities and towns can be harsh. To avoid fines, be informed of where you may and cannot park. Paid parking is enforced in some areas, so keep some change on hand.

9. Thoroughly inspect the vehicle:

Inspect the vehicle for any existing damage before leaving the rental agency. Take note of them and ensure that the rental staff documents them. This helps to avoid disagreements upon return.

Currency and Banking

It is essential to become acquainted with the local currency and banking system when managing your funds in Corsica. Corsica, as a French region, utilizes the Euro (€) as its official currency.This is advantageous for passengers, particularly those arriving from other European countries that utilize the Euro.

Most major credit and debit cards are accepted in most establishments, including hotels, restaurants, and shopping. However, carrying cash is recommended for smaller enterprises or more remote places where card acceptance may be limited.

ATMs are widely available in towns and cities, allowing you to withdraw cash whenever you need it. Inform your bank about your vacation plans ahead of time to avoid any potential problems with card transactions abroad.

Banking hours are largely based on conventional European business hours. Banks are open Monday through Friday, with some closing for a few hours for lunch. It's a good idea to plan ahead of time for your banking needs, especially if you require in-person services.

Currency exchange services are also available, albeit the prices may not be as good as those found at ATMs. If you need to convert money, go to a bank for better rates.

Overall, Corsica has a well-established and convenient financial infrastructure for visitors, making it reasonably simple to manage your finances while on the island. To avoid problems, keep a check on your baggage, utilize secure ATMs, and notify your bank of your vacation plans.

Language Basics: Useful Corsican Phrases

1. **Greetings:**
   - *Bonghjornu* - Good morning
   - *Bona sera* - Good evening
   - *Bona notte* - Good night

2. **Politeness Goes a Long Way:**
   - *Per piacè* - Please
   - *Grazia* - Thank you
   - *Prego* - You're welcome

3. **Getting Around:**
   - *Dove hè...?* - Where is...?
   - *Quantu costa?* - How much does it cost?
   - *Aiutatemi, per piacè* - Help me, please

4. **Foodie Phrases:**
   - *Una tavula per dui* - A table for two
   - *Mi piace assai* - I like it a lot
   - *Un bicchieru di vinu, per piacè* - A glass of wine, please

5. **Emergency Essentials:**
   - *Aiuto!* - Help!
   - *Chjamate i pompieri* - Call the fire brigade

- *Dov'è l'ospedale più vicino?* - Where is the nearest hospital?

Safety Tips for a Hassle-Free Stay

1. Respect the Local Culture:

Corsicans are extremely proud of their distinct culture and traditions. Respecting and being aware of local customs can not only enrich your trip, but will also contribute to positive interactions with the people. Keep in mind that Corsica has its own identity within France, and Corsican is widely spoken alongside French.

2. Nature Caution:

Corsica, with its mountains, forests, and lovely beaches, is a nature lover's heaven. Follow safety precautions when experiencing the great outdoors. If you're going on a hike, make sure you have the proper gear, check the weather, and notify someone of your plans. This is useful in case of unforeseen circumstances.

3. Driving Precautions:

If you plan to tour the island by automobile, keep in mind that Corsican roads can be winding and difficult. Take your time, obey speed restrictions, and exercise caution when driving in mountainous places. Furthermore, some rural roads may be small, so remaining aware is essential.

4. Beach Safety:

Corsica has some of the best beaches in the Mediterranean. Take safety precautions when enjoying the sun and sea. Always swim in specified places, heed local cautions, and be wary of strong currents.

5. Health Preparations:

Make sure you have adequate travel insurance that includes medical coverage. Even if Corsica offers outstanding medical services, it is still a good idea to be prepared. Carry any necessary drugs with you and become acquainted with the location of the nearest pharmacy or medical clinic.

6. Secure Your Belongings:

While Corsica is generally safe, it is prudent to avoid petty thievery. Keep close eye on your belongings, particularly in tourist areas. Keep valuables in hotel safes and avoid exhibiting pricey goods in public.

7. Emergency Response:

Know the emergency phone numbers in your area, including those for medical services and the police. Having these numbers on hand enables a quick response in the event of an emergency.

8. Weather Awareness:

Corsica has a Mediterranean climate, however circumstances might change. Check the weather forecast on a frequent basis, especially if you have plans for outside activities. Weather can change quickly, especially in mountainous areas.

9. Connect with Locals:

Connecting with locals is one of the best methods to be safe. They frequently share significant insights, ranging from hidden gems to local safety recommendations.

Corsica is a beautiful location, and with a little planning and care, you can make the most of your visit while being safe and pleasurable.

Unique town and cities

1. Ajaccio: Napoleon's Hometown

Ajaccio, the capital, is more than a city; it is a trip through time. Stroll around cobblestone lanes where Napoleon Bonaparte once strolled. The Maison Bonaparte, his birthplace, provides an intriguing glimpse into the great French leader's early life.

2. Bonifacio: Clinging to the Cliffs

Bonifacio, a village perched abruptly on limestone cliffs, will charm you. The views of the glistening Mediterranean are magnificent. Explore the Old Town's winding streets, which lead to quaint cafes and stores.

3. Calvi: Citadel by the Sea

Calvi is a postcard-worthy resort, capped by an ancient citadel. The port, which is flanked with colorful eateries, provides the ideal combination of relaxation and culture. The Genoese Citadel, built in the 13th century, is a reminder of Corsica's rich history.

4. Corte: Corsican Heartland

Corte, located in the heart of Corsica, is a symbol of Corsican identity. The Citadel, positioned on a rocky ridge, provides breathtaking views. At the Museum of Corsica, you may immerse yourself in the island's unique heritage.

5. Sartène, Corsica's Most Corsican Town

Sartène, sometimes known as the "Most Corsican of Corsican Towns," is a time capsule of history. Explore the tiny alleyways lined with antique dwellings and pay a visit to the Church of Sainte-Marie for a glimpse of Corsican religious art.

6. Porto-Vecchio's Beaches and More

Porto-Vecchio is the place to go if you want sun-kissed beaches and a lively town feel. The old town is a maze of lovely lanes, while adjacent beaches like Palombaggia and Santa Giulia provide plenty of relaxation.

7. L'Île-Rousse: Seaside Relaxation

L'Île-Rousse is a tranquil beach town called after the red-colored islets off the coast. Place Paoli, with its palm-lined square, is a perfect place to soak in the Corsican way of life. Don't miss the artisan market for handcrafted items from the area.

8. Bastia: Corsica's Northern Gateway

As the northernmost port of entry, Bastia combines a lively harbor with a rich historical past. For a flavor of local life, visit the Terra Vecchia, the old town, and Saint-Nicolas Square.

9. Propriano: Tranquil Seaside Haven

Propriano is a quiet refuge with calm seas and a backdrop of hills. The marina is ideal for long walks, and the neighboring prehistoric site of Filitosa provides an intriguing peek into old Corsican civilization.

10. Centuri: Fishing Village Charms

Centuri is unrivaled for a taste of traditional Corsican fishing village life. This lovely resort is distinguished by charming harbors, seafood restaurants, and the perfume of the sea.

These distinct towns and cities collectively paint Corsica's canvas, each adding its distinctive brushstroke to a work of art of culture, history, and natural beauty.

Top Destinations and Attractions

1. Calvi: A Coastal Treasure

Calvi, located on the northwest coast, is a charming town that mixes traditional beauty with breathtaking scenery. The town's historic citadel, which dates back to the 13th century, offers an insight into Corsica's past, while the pristine beaches provide a peaceful respite. Visitors can stroll through small cobblestone alleyways, visit bustling local markets, and dine on exquisite seafood at seaside eateries.

2. Bonifacio: Cliffs and Citadel

Bonifacio, perched on high limestone cliffs in the island's south, is an intriguing place with a rich history and outstanding natural beauty. The Old Town, positioned on the cliff's edge, provides panoramic views of the Mediterranean Sea. This ancient town has a bustling ambiance thanks to the waterfront, which is surrounded by numerous cafes and shops. Exploring the neighboring sea caves and the Lavezzi Islands by boat is highly recommended.

3. Scandola Nature Reserve: A UNESCO World Heritage Site

The Scandola Nature Reserve, a UNESCO World Heritage site, exemplifies Corsica's natural beauty. This craggy terrain of red cliffs, secret coves, and crystal-clear waters on the western coast is a refuge for nature aficionados. Boat cruises allow visitors to see the diverse marine life, including seals and dolphins, that thrives in the protected waters.

4. Corte: Corsican Heartland

Corte, in the center of the island, is the place to go for a taste of Corsican authenticity. This town, surrounded by mountains, served as Corsica's medieval capital. The magnificent Citadel, which offers panoramic views, is a reminder of Corsica's turbulent past. Visitors can learn about the island's cultural and historical legacy by visiting the Museum of Corsica.

5. Ajaccio: Napoleon's birthplace

Ajaccio, Corsica's city, is not just a busy port but also the birthplace of Napoleon Bonaparte. The Maison Bonaparte, his ancestral home turned museum, provides an intriguing glimpse into the French emperor's early life. The colorful waterfront of the city, with its multitude of cafes and boutiques, is ideal for leisurely strolls and people-watching.

6. The GR20: A Hiker's Paradise

The GR20 is one of Europe's most difficult yet rewarding hiking pathways for adventurers. The trail crosses the island from north to south, passing through a variety of scenery such as woods, mountain lakes, and high-altitude plateaus. While the entire route is a challenge, lesser sections suit to those looking for a day or overnight journey.

7. L'Ile-Rousse: Serene Beauty

L'Ile-Rousse, on the northern coast, is famed for its tranquil atmosphere and red granite beaches. The town's central square, which is lined with palm palms and cafes, is a great place to unwind. L'Ile-Rousse is a perfect destination for anyone looking for a laid-back coastal experience, thanks to its quiet waters and vivid sunsets.

Corsica's numerous attractions cater to a wide range of interests, making it an ideal vacation for anyone looking for a perfect blend of natural beauty, cultural exploration, and outdoor experiences. Corsica delivers a memorable experience, whether you're hiking through rocky mountains, exploring old citadels, or simply relaxing on pristine beaches in the Mediterranean heat.

Exploring Corsica's Picturesque Beaches

1. Palombaggia Beach:

Imagine yourself on a beach with fine, white sand and turquoise waves surrounded by red granite boulders. Palombaggia is for you. This beach, located south of Porto-Vecchio, is well-known for its beautiful scenery, water sports, and lively atmosphere. It's the ideal combination of leisure and recreational activities.

2. Rondinara Beach:

Rondinara Beach, tucked away in a secluded harbor, is widely regarded as one of Corsica's most beautiful. The tranquil, shallow waters are ideal for families, and the surrounding hills create a natural background for a day of sun-soaked bliss.

3. Santa Giulia Beach:

Santa Giulia is a horseshoe-shaped harbor with mild, shallow seas. The beach is surrounded by beautiful hills, making for a peaceful environment for a day at the beach.

From paddleboarding to jet skiing, water sports fans will find enough to do.

4. Saleccia Beach:

Visit Saleccia Beach for a more off-the-beaten-path experience. This beach, accessible only by boat or a strenuous trek, is a hidden gem with beautiful white sand and crystal-clear waters. It's a paradise for nature enthusiasts and those seeking solitude.

5. Ostriconi Beach:

Ostriconi Beach, nestled between the hills and the sea, provides a more raw and natural scene. The beach is framed by dunes and a river, resulting in a one-of-a-kind landscape. It's an excellent alternative for folks who value natural beauty and a sense of remoteness.

Activities for Adventurers

Hiking and Trekking:

Corsica has an extensive network of hiking trails, including the GR20, which is widely regarded as one of Europe's most difficult long-distance treks. The trail passes through a variety of scenery, from lush forests to steep mountains, and offers trekkers beautiful views of the Mediterranean.

Water Sports:

The natural shoreline of the island encourages water enthusiasts to participate in a variety of activities. Scuba diving is especially popular since it allows you to explore vibrant underwater environments. Kayaking and paddleboarding are also good options for exploring Corsica's crystal-clear waterways.

Rock Climbing:

Corsica's hilly environment provides good rock-climbing chances. The Aiguilles de Bavella are a well-known climbing area that offers both obstacles and breathtaking views. Corsica features routes for all skill levels, whether you're a seasoned climber or a beginner.

Canyoning:

Canyoning in Corsica's rocky gorges is a fully immersing adventure. Expert guides take participants through small passages, natural ponds, and waterfalls, producing an amazing combination of trekking, climbing, and swimming.

Paragliding:

Try paragliding to get a bird's-eye perspective of Corsica. The various topography and coastline vistas of the island provide a stunning backdrop for an aerial experience. Tandem flights are provided for beginners, offering a safe and enjoyable experience.

Mountain Biking:

Corsica's varied topography makes it a perfect playground for mountain bikers. The trails range from easy beach pathways to difficult alpine hikes. Explore the island's splendor on two wheels by renting a bike or joining a guided tour.

Adventure Parks:

Visit one of Corsica's treetop adventure parks for a family-friendly excursion. Zip lines, rope bridges, and other obstacles are located among lush forests in these parks, giving a fun and difficult experience for guests of all ages.

Corsica's varied geography guarantees that there is something for everyone, whether you are an experienced thrill seeker or a novice adventurer. You'll discover that the spirit of adventure is strongly rooted in Corsican culture as you explore the island's natural beauties.

Family-Friendly Activities

Beach Vacations:

Corsica has some of the best beaches in the Mediterranean. Palombaggia or Santa Giulia have soft, white sands and clean, shallow seas, making them ideal for a family day out. The beaches provide a variety of water sports and activities for people of all ages.

Historical Exploration:

A visit to the Citadel of Calvi will introduce your family to the history of Corsica. The historic architecture and pirate myths will captivate the children. Exploring the fortress as a group may be both enjoyable and educational.

Hikes and nature trails:

Corsica is a nature lover's delight. Choose family-friendly hiking trails such as the "Sentier des Douaniers" walk along the shore or the "Cascade de Radule" trail, which leads to a beautiful waterfall. Make an adventure out of it by exploring the island's distinctive flora and animals.

Adventure Parks:

Take your family to one of Corsica's adventure parks for an adrenaline experience. In the lush forests of Corsica, tree-climbing courses, zip lines, and obstacle courses await. It's a terrific opportunity for the family to spend time together while enjoying the beautiful outdoors.

Boat Tours and Island Hopping:

A family-friendly boat cruise will allow you to discover Corsica's coastline splendor. Some excursions even include island hopping, allowing your family to see the smaller, less congested islands surrounding Corsica.

Cultural Workshops:

Immerse your family in Corsican culture by participating in interactive activities. Learn traditional Corsican music, dabble in local crafts, or enroll in a culinary class to learn the art of Corsican food. These encounters will leave a lasting impression.

Animal Encounters:

Visit animal sanctuaries and wildlife parks on Corsica, such as the Tortoise Village and the Corsican Nature Reserve. These locations not only provide an educational experience, but also allow your family to interact with the island's distinctive wildlife.

Festivals and Events:

Look for family-friendly festivals and events on the local calendar. Corsicans are known for their boisterous festivities, and taking part in these events will give your family a taste of the island's vivid culture.

Dining on the Beach:

Family lunches can be had at coastal eateries. Corsican food is not only excellent but also suitable for children. The extensive buffet will satisfy everyone's taste buds, with everything from fresh seafood to local cheeses.

Sunset Strolls:

Relax at the end of the day with a stroll along the beach at sunset. The stunning sights and peaceful ambiance make for an ideal family outing.

Corsica offers to a wide range of interests, ensuring that every member of the family enjoys a memorable and pleasurable experience. Corsica provides a family trip unlike any other, whether you're touring historical monuments, participating in water sports, or simply relaxing on the beach.

Local Festivals and Events

1. Corsica's Polyphony Festival:

Corsica is famous for its own style of polyphonic singing known as "Corsican polyphony." Every year, the Polyphony Festival honors this unique music form, attracting musicians and fans from all over the world. The festival is an enthralling excursion into Corsican culture, where traditional tunes mingle with modern influences.

2. Bastia Music Festival:

One of Corsica's largest cities, Bastia, presents an annual Music Festival that features a wide variety of musical styles. This festival highlights the island's diverse cultural influences, ranging from classical symphonies to Corsican folk melodies and worldwide performances.

3. Carnaval de Venise in Corsica:

The famed Venetian Carnival on Corsica is a display of magnificent costumes, masks, and vibrant parades. This celebration in Sartène mixes Venetian charm into Corsican customs, resulting in a visually magnificent and culturally complex experience.

4. Calvi Jazz Festival:

The Calvi Jazz Festival is a must-attend event for jazz fans. Famous jazz performers create an amazing mood against the backdrop of the citadel, which resonates with both locals and visitors. This festival is a lovely celebration of jazz notes and Corsican hospitality.

5. A Filetta Concerts:

A Filetta, a Corsican singing group known for their polyphonic chants, plays frequently on the island. Attending one of their concerts gives you a real and intimate taste of Corsican music, with haunting harmonies echoing through historic cathedrals or stunning outdoor venues.

6. Chestnut Festivals:

Autumn ushers forth a flurry of chestnut festivities across Corsica, honoring the island's chestnut groves. Local artisans, traditional music, and, of course, a variety of chestnut-based foods are included at these festivals. It's a fantastic opportunity to sample unique Corsican dishes while taking in the autumn celebrations.

7. Corpus Domini Procession:

The Corpus Domini procession is a prominent religious festival in the town of Cargèse. This serious but beautiful parade winds through the streets, displaying Corsican religious traditions as well as the close-knit communal spirit.

8. Sant'Andrea di Cotone:

In July, the Sant'Andrea di Cotone festival is a colorful celebration of Corsican heritage. Traditional Corsican clothes, music, and dance can be seen by visitors, presenting a vivid portrait of the island's cultural character.

Exploring Corsica during these festivals and events provides tourists with an exceptional and immersive view of the island's rich cultural tapestry.

Traditional Corsican Music and Dance

Corsican music reflects the island's distinct history and cultural influences. Corsican melodies cannot be studied without encountering the polyphonic singing technique known as "A Cappella." This traditional style of vocal music frequently employs three or four-part harmonies, resulting in a hauntingly beautiful and distinct sound.

Polyphonic singing acts as a sound time capsule, preserving the stories of Corsica's struggle, tenacity, and beauty. The lyrics expertly weave themes of love, nature, and historical events, providing a lyrical glimpse into the Corsican way of life.

Instruments like the cetera, a traditional Corsican lute, and the pifana, a type of flute, add layers to the musical landscape. These instruments, when paired with the powerful vocals of Corsican singers, provide an audio experience that both locals and visitors enjoy.

To properly appreciate Corsican culture, one must participate in the island's traditional dances. Corsican dances are a vibrant representation of the people's happiness, tenacity, and communal spirit.

One of the most well-known dances is the "Saltarello." This energetic and rhythmic dance with sophisticated footwork and quick motions originated in the medieval courts. Dancers frequently form circles or lines, which adds to the communal atmosphere of the performance.

Another prominent sight at Corsican celebrations is the "Cercle," or circle dance. This dance is frequently performed in conjunction with festivities and events, giving a sense of solidarity and shared joy among participants.

Corsican festivals and local gatherings are excellent places to experience the enchantment of traditional music and dance. The "Calvi Jazz Festival" and the "Rencontres de Chants Polyphoniques" in Calvi are both noteworthy events that highlight Corsican musical tradition.

Furthermore, smaller villages frequently organize local gatherings with traditional entertainment. The sincerity and passion of Corsican music and dance shine through in these small settings.

Whether in a bustling town square or a sleepy village, the essence of Corsican culture is emphasized by lyrical tunes and rhythmic dances passed down through generations. These cultural displays are more than just performances; they are live, breathing traditions that connect the past with the present, transforming Corsica into a destination where history and artistry meet.

Must-Try Corsican Dishes

1. Fiadone

Fiadone is a traditional Corsican dessert that begins sweet. It's a cheesecake-like delicacy cooked with brocciu, a fresh cheese that's synonymous with Corsican cuisine. Its creamy texture and delicate sweetness make it the ideal complement to any Corsican dinner.

2. Figatellu:

Figatellu is a must-try for individuals who enjoy savory treats. This Corsican sausage is often made with pork and liver and is seasoned with a variety of aromatic herbs. The distinct flavors reflect the island's agricultural background.

3. Wild Boar:

The rocky environment of Corsica has shaped not only its terrain but also its culinary offerings. Wild boar appears frequently in Corsican menus, prepared in a variety of ways. The powerful flavor represents the untamed essence of the island, from slow-cooked stews to grilled specialties.

4. Brocciu:

Brocciu deserves to be singled out. This adaptable cheese can be found in both sweet and savory dishes. It conveys the essence of Corsican dairy craftsmanship whether crumbled over spaghetti or coupled with honey in a dessert.

5. Civet de Sanglier:

Civet de Sanglier, or wild boar stew, is a substantial dish that captures the flavors of Corsica. Slow-cooked to perfection, it exemplifies the island's skill in transforming game meats into gourmet wonders.

6. Accenti:

Accenti, a meal that blends fresh fish with local herbs and spices, will delight seafood lovers. Because of its proximity to the Mediterranean, Corsican seafood is not only abundant but also extremely fresh.

7. Canistrelli:

No culinary adventure is complete without a dash of sweetness. Canistrelli, or Corsican biscuits, are the ideal treat for individuals who enjoy sweets. These crunchy treats, which are sometimes flavored with anise or chestnut flour, go perfectly with a cup of Corsican coffee.

Each meal in Corsica tells a story, weaving together threads of history, geography, and culture. The island's food, like the Corsican people, demonstrates the island's tenacity and adaptability.

Nightlife and Entertainment

Ajaccio, the capital, comes alive at night with its marina-front bars and pubs. Visit the Old Town to locate historic taverns like Bar de la Fossette, where you may sip a Corsican beer while admiring centuries-old architecture. The palm-lined marina provides a lovely setting for a leisurely evening stroll.

Calvi is well-known for its beach parties and upscale waterfront restaurants. Explore Quai Landry, where seaside bars like U Fanale offer the right combination of tranquility and exciting entertainment. The sea breeze and the sound of the waves add to the atmosphere, making it a one-of-a-kind Corsican experience.

With its multicultural atmosphere, Bastia has a diversified nightlife. Terra Nova is known for its sophisticated cocktail lounges and dancing clubs. Local music is celebrated at venues such as L'Aliva, where you can groove to traditional Corsican tunes mixed with modern sounds.

Bonifacio has a more laid-back yet equally enchanting nightlife. For sunset cocktails and breathtaking views of the Mediterranean, visit cliffside bars like Santa Manza. The relaxed atmosphere makes it a great place to unwind after a day of exploring.

The nightlife of Porto-Vecchio concentrates around its exquisite beach clubs and stylish nightclubs. Perched on the hills, Le Roof Lounge provides a stylish environment with live music and a broad beverage menu. The beach clubs on Palombaggia Beach have a sophisticated and energetic vibe.

Corte, home to Corsica's university, has a youthful energy. Explore Rue Cesar Campinchi for student-friendly bars such as U Museu, where you can socialize with locals while sipping Corsican wines. The colorful ambiance of the town provides a unique peek into Corsican student life.

Corsica's festivals, while not traditional nightclubs, are a must-see. The Calvi Jazz Festival and Porto Latino Festival combine music, dance, and traditional Corsican food to create a colorful celebration of Corsican culture. Check the calendar for events taking place during your visit.\

Corsica's nightlife culture is as varied as its scenery, ensuring that every visitor finds an experience that suits their tastes. The island's entertainment options reflect its diverse cultural tapestry, ranging from medieval pubs to seaside celebrations. Corsica delivers wonderful evenings imbued with Mediterranean flair, whether you enjoy sipping cocktails by the sea or dancing to local beats.

10 Best Nightclubs and Bars

1. **Chez Tao (Ajaccio):** Chez Tao is a sophisticated nightclub in the heart of Ajaccio that offers a variety of music genres. It caters to a varied audience with anything from throbbing modern beats to classic tunes. The outside terrace offers a spectacular view of the city lights.

2. **Bar de la Plage (Calvi):** Located directly on the beach in Calvi, Bar de la Plage is the ideal place to relax with a cocktail in hand. Waves compliment the music, creating a relaxed yet energetic mood.

3. **U Santa Marina (Bonifacio):** U Santa Marina in Bonifacio is a must-see for a taste of Corsican culture. The traditional décor, live music, and vast selection of Corsican wines make it a one-of-a-kind and unforgettable experience.

4. **Les 3 Terrasses (Bastia):** Overlooking Bastia's Old Port, Les 3 Terrasses is a trendy venue serving craft

beers and drinks. The terrace has a great view of the port and is popular with both locals and tourists.

5. **Le B52 (Porto-Vecchio):** If you're looking for a place to dance, Le B52 in Porto-Vecchio is the place to go. It's a magnet for people looking to dance the night away, with themed parties and a bustling atmosphere.

6. **A Scudella (Corte):** A Scudella in Corte provides a warm and personal atmosphere. This tavern, known for its artisan beers and local wines, is popular among students and locals, providing a cheerful and welcoming atmosphere.

7. **Via Notte (Porto-Vecchio):** As one of Europe's largest nightclubs, Via Notte provides an extravagant experience. With many dance floors and renowned DJs, it draws partygoers from all over the world.

8. **Lounge Bar L'Alivu (Ile-Rousse):** For a more leisurely evening, visit to Ile-Rousse's Lounge Bar L'Alivu. The relaxing atmosphere, comfy seats, and wide beverage menu make it a great location to unwind.

9. **U Spuntinu (Ajaccio):** This quaint wine bar in Ajaccio serves a variety of local wines as well as delectable tapas. The welcoming atmosphere and skilled personnel make it an excellent place to learn about Corsican wine culture.

10. **Le Piano Chez Toinou (Bastia):** If you enjoy live music, head to Le Piano Chez Toinou in Bastia. It's a favorite among music fans, with regular live performances ranging from jazz to rock.

Remember that Corsica's nightlife culture is as diverse as the island itself. Corsica has something for everyone, whether you want electronic sounds, live music, or a peaceful drink by the beach.

Packing Essentials: What to Bring to Corsica

When packing for your Corsican excursion, make sure you have everything you'll need for a comfortable and enjoyable trip. Corsica's varied landscapes, from harsh mountains to pristine beaches, necessitate an adaptable wardrobe as well as a few specific items to make the most of your visit.

Comfortable Footwear:

The terrain on Corsica can be rather varied, so bring strong and comfortable footwear. A good pair of hiking boots is essential if you intend to visit the hiking routes or mountainous regions. Don't forget flip-flops or comfy sandals for beach days.

Light Clothing:

Corsica's Mediterranean climate means hot, dry summers. To keep cool during the day, bring light, breathable clothing. A hat and sunglasses are also recommended to protect yourself from the sun.

Swimwear:

Because Corsica has some of the most gorgeous beaches in the Mediterranean, bring your swimsuit. You'll want to take advantage of the crystal-clear waters whether you're into snorkeling, sunbathing, or water sports.

Weather-Appropriate Layers:

Evenings can be cool, particularly in mountainous places. Bring a light jacket or sweater for cooler nights, and consider bringing a waterproof layer in case of rain.

Daypack for Exploring:

Corsica is a sanctuary for outdoor enthusiasts, so a daypack will come in handy for your excursions. As you venture out to explore the island, pack some food, a water bottle, sunscreen, and a map.

Power Adapters:

Bring the necessary power adapters to keep your electrical devices charged. Corsica, as part of France, primarily uses Type E sockets, thus bring the appropriate plugs.

Medical Kit:

It's usually a good idea to keep a basic medical kit on hand. Include pain remedies, sticky bandages, any prescription drugs, and seasickness tablets if you intend to travel by boat.

Reusable Water Bottle:

Staying hydrated is critical, especially if you're doing outside activities. Bring a reusable water bottle to decrease plastic waste and guarantee you always have water readily hand.

Language App or Phrasebook:

While French is the official language, Corsican, a distinct Romance language, is spoken by many Corsicans. Understanding common terms can improve your experience and relationships with locals.

Travel Documents:

Don't forget your passport, travel insurance, and any necessary visas. It's also a good idea to have paper or digital copies of your reservations, as well as a map of the island.

You'll be well-equipped to make the most of your time on this gorgeous Mediterranean island if you pack intelligently and prepare for Corsica's numerous options.

Best Times to Visit

Corsica's Mediterranean environment makes it an enticing vacation practically all year. The sweet spot, however, is often from late spring to early autumn, or from May to October. Temperatures range between 20 and 30 degrees Celsius (68- and 86-degrees Fahrenheit) during these months. This is when the island truly comes to life, and you can enjoy the full range of Corsica's offerings.

May and June are particularly lovely. Wildflowers litter the island, and the countryside is a pallet of greens and yellows. The weather is ideal for visiting old villages, trekking in the mountains, or relaxing on one of the many gorgeous beaches. Nature is regenerating, and the sense of vigor pervades the air.

Summer officially begins in July and August. The beaches are crowded, the sea is warm, and the events are in full flow. Corsica has a rich cultural legacy, and you can hear traditional music, dancing, and other celebrations that highlight the island's unique personality during these months.

Try the shoulder seasons of September and October if you prefer a calmer experience with still-warm temps. The summer throngs have thinned down, but the weather remains lovely. It's a great time for people who wish to explore the sceneries, learn about the local culture, and sample the cuisine without the congestion and bustle of peak tourist season.

If you want to experience the classic Mediterranean sun and sand, you should avoid the winter months. While the island does not close, many coastal enterprises close during this time.

In essence, the best time to visit Corsica is determined by your personal preferences. Corsica has a season for everyone, whether you're looking for sun, culture, or adventure.

Accommodation Guide

When it comes to finding the perfect place to stay in Corsica, you're in for a treat. The island has a broad choice of hotel alternatives that appeal to all preferences and budgets, ensuring that every guest has a comfortable and pleasurable stay.

Corsica has an array of expensive hotels and resorts that combine breathtaking vistas with top-notch amenities for visitors seeking a touch of luxury. Imagine waking up to the sound of waves and magnificent vistas of the Mediterranean Sea. These places frequently have fine dining options, wellness facilities, and private beaches, offering a true experience of luxury.

Consider staying in a nice bed & breakfast or a guesthouse if you want to immerse yourself in the local culture. Corsican hospitality is legendary, and these places let you experience it for yourself. You'll most likely be surrounded by rustic charm, with hosts ready to impart information about the island's history, traditions, and hidden gems.

Corsica also has a variety of cheap options for the budget-conscious traveler. Hostels and inexpensive motels may be found all throughout the island, offering clean and minimal services to people who would rather spend their money touring the island than on lodging.

The presence of gîtes is a distinctive feature of Corsican housing. These are typically vacation homes or cottages in lovely rural surroundings. Staying in a gîte gives you the independence of self-catering accommodation while also giving a home away from home. It's a wonderful choice for anyone wishing to get away from it all and enjoy the peace and quiet of Corsica's countryside.

Consider staying in an agriturismo to fully connect with the island. These are operating farms that provide lodging for visitors. Imagine waking up to the aroma of blooming flowers in the midst of vineyards or olive orchards. Agriturismos offer a genuine experience, allowing you to appreciate locally made cuisine and wine while taking in the rustic charm of the Corsican countryside.

It is best to schedule your Corsican vacation well in advance, especially during the peak tourist season. This guarantees that you have a variety of options to select from and that you can acquire the type of lodging that best suits your needs.

Corsica's numerous accommodation offers ensure a memorable and pleasant stay on this fascinating island, whether you choose a magnificent coastal resort, a quaint bed and breakfast, or a charming gîte in the mountains.

10 Best Accommodation Options

1. Hotel La Villa

Location: Calvi

Hotel La Villa, located in the heart of Calvi, offers spectacular views of the bay. It's ideal for anyone looking for a little extravagance, with its opulent accommodations, spa, and Michelin-starred restaurant.

2. U Capu Biancu

Location: Bonifacio

U Capu Biancu, perched on the cliffs overlooking the Mediterranean, provides a private and romantic hideaway. Couples will enjoy the private beach and excellent seafood.

3. Hotel Genovese

Location: Bonifacio

Hotel Genovese, located within the medieval citadel, blends charm and history. The panoramic terrace provides breathtaking sunset views, making it a favorite among people who value authenticity.

4. A Cheda

Location: Bonifacio

A Cheda is a hidden treasure in Corsica, surrounded by lovely gardens. The spacious rooms and outdoor pool create a relaxing atmosphere, making it a great place to unwind after a day of exploring.

5. La Dimora

Location: Corte

Dimora, located in the heart of Corsica's mountainous core, offers a rustic yet beautiful experience. Its proximity to Corte's cultural treasures makes it an excellent choice for history buffs.

6. Hotel Misincu

Location: Macinaggio

Hotel Misincu, located near Macinaggio's marina, combines elegance and nature. The accommodations with sea views and the organic restaurant highlight Corsica's natural charm.

7. Dominique Colonna

Location: Corte

Dominique Colonna, located on the Tavignano River, is a nature lover's dream. The wooden cabins and calm surroundings make it a popular destination for hikers and outdoor enthusiasts.

8. Les Bergeries de Palombaggia

Location: Porto-Vecchio

This beautiful hostel overlooks the famed Palombaggia beach and embodies Corsican hospitality. The proximity to the beach, as well as the lush grounds, contribute to the tranquil mood.

9. Hotel Carre Noir

Location: Porto-Vecchio

Hotel Carre Noir, located in the heart of Porto-Vecchio, mixes modern comfort with Corsican originality. The rooftop pool provides breathtaking views of the town and neighboring hills.

10. Hotel Cala di Greco
Location: Bonifacio

Located on the cliffs of Bonifacio, Hotel Cala di Greco offers a magnificent retreat. The infinity pool and modern rooms make it a popular choice for visitors looking for a combination of refinement and natural beauty.

These suggestions cater to a wide range of tastes, from seaside luxury to mountain getaways, ensuring that every visitor finds their ideal sanctuary in Corsica.

Souvenirs and Local Treasures

You're in for a treat when it comes to souvenirs and local gems in Corsica. With its rich history and colorful culture, this enchanting island provides a wealth of one-of-a-kind goods that make ideal memories of your Corsican experience.

Corsican Charcuterie:

Corsica is famous for its charcuterie, notably its cured meats. Get some lonzu (cured pig loin) or figatellu (smoked liver sausage) from your local market. These delicacies are not only delicious, but they also represent a piece of Corsican culinary culture.

Corsican Cheese:

Cheese connoisseurs will enjoy Corsica's range of artisanal cheeses. Brocciu, a fresh goat or sheep milk cheese, is a must-try. It's adaptable, as it can be used in both sweet and savory dishes, and it embodies the island's pastoral background.

Corsican Wines:

Corsican wines are an undiscovered treasure. Vineyards on the island produce distinctive varieties such as Sciaccarellu and Niellucciu. A bottle of Corsican wine is more than simply a drink; it's a taste of the island's terroir and a wonderful way to recall the breathtaking scenery.

Essential Oils from Corsica:

Corsica's rich vegetation produces scented plants such as immortelle and myrtle. Essential oils extracted from these plants are frequently available in local markets. A little vial can serve as a fragrant memory of the natural beauty of the island.

Corsican Pottery:

Corsican artisanal pottery is not only visually stunning, but it embodies a feeling of Corsican artistry. Plates, bowls, and ornamental items embellished with traditional Corsican patterns create memorable keepsakes.

Knives from Corsica:

Corsican knives, particularly the legendary Corsican Vendetta knife, serve a dual purpose. These handcrafted blades are frequently ornately adorned and symbolize Corsican craftsmanship.

Corsican Scents Inspired Perfumes:

Many local perfumers have been influenced by Corsica's aromatic terrain, which is dotted with maquis plants and lemon trees. Consider purchasing a perfume that encapsulates the spirit of Corsica, allowing you to carry a scent of the island with you.

Honey from Corsica:

Corsican honey is a pleasant and natural memento made from the island's various flora. The distinct flavors obtained by herbs such as chestnut or thyme make it a delectable complement to your culinary repertoire.

Corsican Chestnut Products:

Corsica is famous for its chestnut orchards, and there are many chestnut-based items available. These dishes, ranging from chestnut flour to chestnut cream, demonstrate Corsica's gastronomic versatility.

Corsican Handmade Soaps:

Handmade soaps combined with local herbs and scents provide a useful yet enjoyable keepsake. They frequently show the island's dedication to natural and traditional items.

Remember that each of these treasures not only acts as a memento of your Corsican adventure, but also helps to preserve and celebrate the island's cultural history.

Best Shopping Spots for Authentic Local Gifts

Bastia's Market Square: The Market Square in Bastia, in northern Corsica, offers a variety shopping experience. Explore the stalls for local products, handcrafted crafts, and one-of-a-kind Corsican treasures.

Artè Boutique in Ajaccio: Artè Boutique in Ajaccio is a creative paradise for anyone interested in art and design. It has a curated assortment of local artwork, jewelry, and home decor, making it an excellent place to find unique presents.

Craft Market on L'Île-Rousse: L'Île-Rousse holds a lovely craft market where local artisans showcase their talents. It's a terrific place to find unique products like Corsican-themed pottery and handcrafted soaps.

Calvi's Citadel Boutiques: The charming town of Calvi, with its historic citadel, boasts a selection of boutiques selling high-quality Corsican products. These businesses give a taste of the island's natural riches, from scented plants to locally produced honey.

Propriano's Seafront Shops: Propriano, with its inviting seafront, is home to shops that showcase Corsican fashion and accessories. As a fashionable reminder of your trip, purchase a stylish piece of apparel or a locally designed accessory.

Galerie la Grotte in Porto-Vecchio: If you like art, you should go to Galerie la Grotte in Porto-Vecchio. This gallery exhibits Corsican modern art, including as paintings, sculptures, and photography.

Bonifacio's Old Town Market: Perched on stunning cliffs, Bonifacio's Old Town features a dynamic market where local artists sell their wares. This market is a treasure resource for one-of-a-kind souvenirs, with everything from scented Corsican cheeses to handcrafted jewelry.

Ajaccio's Rue Fesch: For a taste of urban shopping, head to Rue Fesch in Ajaccio. This lively street is dotted with businesses selling Corsican specialties such as olive oil, wine, and distinctive Corsican knives known as "couteaux."

Sartène's Sunday Market: Don't miss Sartène's market if you're in Corsica on a Sunday. Stalls offering local vegetables, crafts, and apparel bring life to this charming village. It's a fantastic opportunity to meet people and learn about Corsican culture.

Corte's Artisan Boutiques: Corte, located in the heart of Corsica, is well-known for its handcrafted boutiques. Handcrafted things such as pottery, leather goods, and textiles can be found here. The artistry of these objects reflects the town's rich cultural past.

Each of these locations not only allows you to shop but also immerses you in Corsica's colorful local culture.

7 days Itinerary for an Outdoor/Adventure Enthusiast

Day 1: Arrival in Ajaccio

Begin your journey at Ajaccio, Corsica's capital. Explore the historic old town, pay a visit to Napoleon's birthplace, and spend the evening relaxing on the Gulf of Ajaccio. For a taste of what's to come, try Corsican cuisine at a local restaurant.

Day 2: Lovely Drive to Calvi

Hire a car and take a lovely trip to Calvi. The road offers beautiful views of the seashore and hilly scenery. Wander through the lovely alleyways of Calvi's ancient town and relax on the sandy beaches upon arrival.

Day 3: Hiking in Calanche de Piana

Prepare for a day of hiking in the breathtaking Calanche de Piana. This is a photographer's dream because to the red granite cliffs and crystal-clear seas. Choose a track that is appropriate for your level of fitness and immerse yourself in Corsica's natural splendor.

Day 4: Canyoning Adventure in Restonica Valley

Travel to Corte, Corsica's heart, for a spectacular canyoning excursion in Restonica Valley. You'll navigate around rock formations and plunge into natural pools surrounded by granite mountains—an adrenaline-pumping experience.

Day 5: Sail to the Lavezzi Islands

A sailing vacation to the Lavezzi Islands is a great way to get away from the land. Snorkel in clear waters, discover scenic beaches, and dine on board. Corsica's pristine beauty is reflected in its marine life and untouched landscapes.

Day 6: Mountain Biking in Alta Rocca

Explore the rugged hills of Alta Rocca for a change of pace. Rent a mountain bike and ride into the woods. Stop by Zonza for a sampling of local cheeses and cured meats—an excellent way to refuel.

Day 7: Rest and relaxation in Porto-Vecchio

Finish your journey with a day of relaxation at Porto-Vecchio. Explore the town's historic core, savor local cuisine, and relax on the beautiful Palombaggia Beach. It's the ideal way to round off a week full with Corsican beauties.

Remember that the allure of Corsica rests not only in its landscapes, but also in the friendliness of its people and the richness of its traditions. Adjust the route to your liking and let Corsica's daring spirit enchant you.

7 Days Itinerary for Family Travel

The island has the ideal combination of natural beauty, historical monuments, and family-friendly activities. Let's go over each day in detail so you can get the most of your Corsican journey.

Day 1: Arrival in Ajaccio

Begin your tour at Ajaccio, Corsica's capital. After settling up, take a leisurely stroll around the palm-lined lanes of the old town. Explore the bustling local markets and the Maison Bonaparte, Napoleon Bonaparte's birthplace. In the evening, dine on Corsican cuisine in a family-friendly establishment.

Day 2: Explore Ajaccio's Beaches

Ajaccio, like the rest of Corsica, has beautiful beaches. Spend the day relaxing at Plage Saint-François or Trottel Beach, where your children can play in the shallow water while you relax. Visit the Parc de la Tête d'Or in the afternoon, a nice park with playgrounds for youngsters.

Day 3: Head to Calvi

Visit Calvi, a lovely town on Italy's northwest coast. Explore the Citadel, which provides panoramic views of the city and the sea. Calvi is famed for its lovely beaches, so spend the afternoon creating sandcastles and enjoying the weather at Calvi Beach.

Day 4: A Mountain Adventure

Get away from the beaches and explore the mountains. For a family-friendly hike, visit Restonica Valley. The environment is stunning, and you may choose a course that is appropriate for your family's fitness level. Enjoy a picnic in the midst of nature.

Day 5: Beautiful Drive to Bonifacio

Drive across the countryside to Bonifacio, a lovely cliffside town in the south. Visit King Aragon's staircase and enjoy a boat journey to the sea caverns while exploring the ancient Old Town. There are numerous family-friendly eateries with spectacular views in Bonifacio.

Day 6: Unwind at Palombaggia Beach

Spend the day lounging at Palombaggia Beach, which is famed for its clean seas and white sand. The shallow water is ideal for children, and the beach is flanked by pine trees, which provide natural shade. Enjoy water activities or simply relax on the beach.

Day 7: Departure

Consider paying a morning visit to the Aiguilles de Bavella, which are beautiful needle-like rock formations. After that, depending on your departure schedule, you may do some last-minute souvenir shopping in Porto-Vecchio before saying farewell to Corsica.

This itinerary combines the finest of Corsica's landscapes, history, and family-friendly attractions, ensuring that everyone in the family has an outstanding time.

Romantic/Honeymoon Itinerary

Corsica, located in the center of the Mediterranean, offers a distinct cultural tapestry as well as natural beauty, making it a perfect destination for romantic getaways and honeymoons. Here's a romantic schedule to make your getaway genuinely unforgettable.

Day 1: Arrival in Bastia

Begin your romantic adventure at Bastia, Corsica's main harbor city. Hand in hand, stroll through the small lanes of the old town, discovering exquisite cafes and boutiques. Spend a romantic evening in a local restaurant, savoring Corsican delicacies and taking in the lively environment.

Day 2: Beautiful Drive to Cap Corse

Take a lovely journey to Cap Corse, the picturesque peninsula at Corsica's northern point. Nonza, a hamlet set on spectacular cliffs with breathtaking views of the Mediterranean, is a must-see. Relax with a leisurely seaside meal at one of the charming coastal restaurants.

Day 3: Calvi Relaxation

Visit Calvi, a charming town with a crescent-shaped bay. Spend the day relaxing on the sands or exploring the old Citadel. Take a sunset stroll down the promenade in the evening, followed by a romantic meal overlooking the harbor.

Day 4: Corsican Wine Tasting

Corsica is famous for its wine, and what better way to commemorate romance than with a wine-tasting tour? Indulge in the aromas of Corsican wines from local vineyards in the Balagne region. Choose a bottle to enjoy later when the sun sets beyond the horizon.

Day 5: Spelunca Gorge Adventure

Enter the rocky Spelunca Gorge for a taste of adventure. Hike through this natural beauty, surrounded by high cliffs and a green landscape, with your partner. The Gorge leads to Evisa, a beautiful village where you can enjoy a quiet lunch at a rustic mountain inn.

Day 6: Bonifacio Cliffside Glamour

Discover the lovely village of Bonifacio on Corsica's southern edge. Bonifacio, perched on rocks high above the sea, offers breathtaking views and a romantic setting. Wander through the small streets of the ancient town and take a boat cruise to see the stunning cliffs from below.

Day 7: Porto-Vecchio Relaxation Day

Spend your final full day at Porto-Vecchio, which is noted for its gorgeous beaches and pristine waters. Relax on the sandy beaches or go on a boat cruise to discover hidden coves. Finish your romantic getaway with a candlelit meal to commemorate your time together in this Mediterranean paradise.

Corsica's romantic attractiveness stems from its various scenery, ancient charm, and welcoming people. This itinerary is designed to capture the essence of Corsica, offering the ideal setting for creating memorable memories with your loved one.

The Best Booking Resources

Booking.com: Known for its enormous database of lodgings worldwide, Booking.com is a popular destination for many visitors to Corsica. Booking.com offers to a wide range of interests and budgets, from boutique hotels overlooking the turquoise Mediterranean to quaint bed & breakfasts hidden in the heart of lovely communities.

Airbnb: For a more customized experience, travelers can interact with locals and stay in unique apartments through Airbnb. In Corsica, this may be a charming mountain house or a seaside condominium with panoramic views. It's a wonderful choice for anyone looking for a true Corsican experience.

Expedia: With a wide range of alternatives, Expedia is a dependable resource for booking not only lodging but also flights and vehicle rentals. Their simple platform makes it simple to bundle your travel necessities and save both time and money.

Corsican Hotel Websites: Many hotels and resorts in Corsica have their own websites where you can book directly. This not only ensures that you receive correct information about the hotel, but it may also include exclusive pricing or rewards for booking directly.

Local Travel Agencies: Especially if you're planning a package deal that includes flights, accommodation, and possibly tours, local travel agencies can be valuable. They frequently have firsthand knowledge of the best places to stay and may offer a more personalized booking experience.

Travel Forums and Blogs: Before making a final decision, check out travel forums and blogs for firsthand accounts and advice from other travelers. They can provide insights on hidden gems as well as recommendations for the best places to stay.

Remember that due to Corsica's prominence as a tourist destination, rooms might fill up rapidly, especially during peak seasons. It's best to reserve ahead of time, especially if you have a specific location or style of lodging in mind.

Travelers can assure a comfortable and enjoyable stay in Corsica by utilizing these tools, locating accommodations that suit their interests and budget while immersing themselves in the island's rich history and natural beauty.

Conclusion

As your Corsica travel comes to an end, take a moment to reflect on the island's distinct charm and numerous options. Corsica, with its rocky scenery, rich culture, and kind hospitality, leaves an indelible impression on any traveler who is fortunate enough to discover its wonders.

This island welcomes you not just with an azure sea and golden beaches, but also with a rich tapestry of history and traditions. Corsica's distinct blend of French and Italian influences can be found in many aspects of life, from its language to its food.

You've seen the dramatic shift from the mountainous interior, a paradise for hikers and environment enthusiasts, to the sun-kissed coastal districts with their stunning beaches while navigating the island's terrain. The variety of scenery demonstrates Corsica's capacity to accommodate to a wide range of vacation interests.

No trip to Corsica would be complete without sampling the island's delectable cuisine. The food of the island reflects its terroir, with indigenous ingredients taking center stage. Every meal is a voyage through Corsican food, from the delicious charcuterie to the delightful cheeses. Make sure to sample the unique Corsican wines that match the local cuisine.

Your tour has also highlighted the significance of cultural etiquette, as respecting Corsican traditions and beliefs is essential to having a genuinely immersive experience. Learning a few Corsican phrases, participating in local events, and enjoying the hospitality of the locals will surely enrich your stay.

Transportation and lodging are critical components of a smooth vacation experience. The island's well-connected highways make navigation simple, and a range of housing options suit to every taste, whether you desire the rustic charm of a mountain inn or the opulence of a beach resort.

As your tour guide draws to a close, it's evident that Corsica is more than simply a destination; it's a tapestry of experiences waiting to be woven into your trip memories. Corsica welcomes you with open arms, whether you're an adventurer looking for mountain routes, a family looking for sun-soaked beaches, or a culture enthusiast immersing yourself in local traditions.

Corsica's wild beauty begs you to discover its secret nooks and enjoy the essence of "L'île de Beauté" - the Island of Beauty. May your Corsican experience be full with amazing moments, and may the essence of this enchanting island stay with you long after your visit is over.